Cornwall's Lost Railways

by
Peter Dale

Station and Hotel, Padstow.

Padstow Station and the Metropole Hotel, c.1902.

© Peter Dale, 2001
First published in the United Kingdom, 2001,
by Stenlake Publishing, Ochiltree Sawmill, The Lade,
Ochiltree, Ayrshire, KA18 2NX
Telephone/Fax: 01290 423114
enquiries@stenlake.co.uk
www.stenlake.co.uk

ISBN 1 84033 145 3

ACKNOWLEDGMENTS

I would like to thank my father for getting me started in this wonderful hobby many years ago, and also Ken Jones for introducing me to this project.

The publishers wish to thank John Alsop for permission to reproduce the photographs on the front cover, the inside front cover, pages 1–13, 15–18, 20, 21, 23–39, 41–43, 45–48, the inside back cover and the back cover; and Neville Stead for pages 14 (photograph by B.G. Tweed), 19 (photograph by B.G. Tweed), 22, 40 and 44.

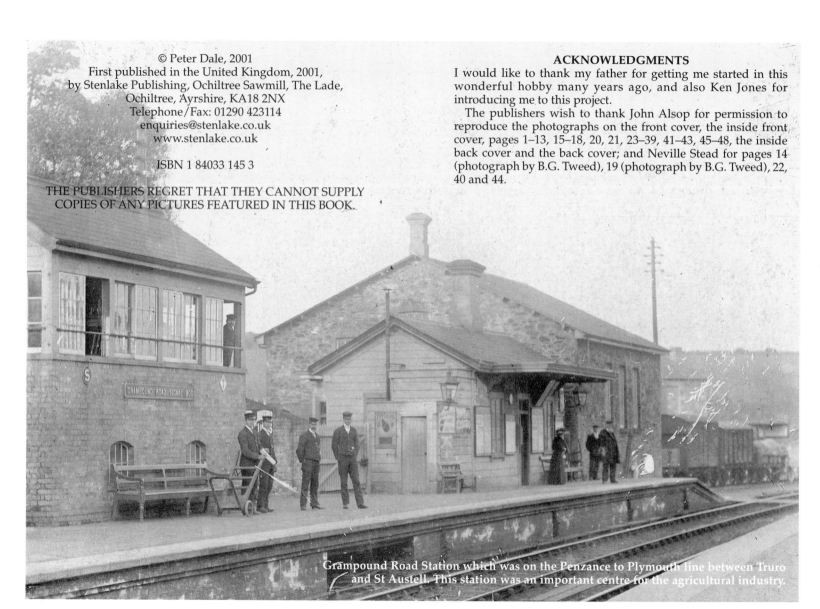

Grampound Road Station which was on the Penzance to Plymouth line between Truro and St Austell. This station was an important centre for the agricultural industry.

INTRODUCTION

Today Cornwall is often thought of as a holiday destination or a bucolic, rural county, but two hundred years ago it was in the forefront of the Industrial Revolution, spurred on by the needs of the copper and tin mining industry. Indeed a Cornishman, Richard Trevithick, built the first steam railway locomotive 25 years before Stephenson's Rocket. He also later built what was probably the world's first pleasure rail line, which ran in London in 1808. The earliest lines in the county were of the plateway type (where the wheels of the carriages were not flanged and the rails, or plates, typically of about 3 feet in length, were cast in an L-section). The first of these, the Poldice Tramway, was open by 1812; this line did not carry passengers officially, but it had a carriage to convey the directors.

The county was dominated by two pre-Grouping companies, the London & South Western Railway (LSWR) in the north eastern part, and the Great Western Railway (GWR) in the rest. The Great Western was built to a broad gauge of 7 feet and its connection, the Cornwall Railway from Plymouth to Falmouth, followed suit. One line, the West Cornwall, started life as a standard gauge line, but when it was linked to the rest of the broad gauge system, a third rail was added to facilitate through running of trains from Paddington to Penzance. The Great Western lost the 'Battle of the Gauges' and the last 7 feet gauge express ran in May 1892. In the twentieth century both the LSWR and GWR sought to develop the area, with its milder climate, for holidaymakers. This came at a time when the traditional industries in the area were in decline and changing work patterns meant more people had paid holidays.

Helston Station. As one of the new motor buses is in the station yard (left) this picture is dated between 1903 and 1908 when the GWR introduced a single colour 'chocolate lake' coach livery. It did not start to reinstate the famous chocolate and cream livery until 1922.

Shortly after the new century began the GWR introduced its first bus service which ran from Helston to The Lizard. These new contraptions put paid to proposals for light railways to The Lizard and from Penzance to Land's End and St Just.

In 1923 the old railway companies were grouped into four. In Cornwall the LSWR became part of the Southern Railway, while the GWR continued, having been enlarged by absorption of a number of smaller lines, many in Wales. While the railways continued to increase the numbers of holidaymakers coming to Cornwall, road competition now became significant for the first time. Despite this, most lines continued through nationalisation in 1948 and until the Beeching era of the early 1960s. Under Beeching's plans many Cornish branches were due to close and, at one time, the mainline from Plymouth to Penzance was itself under threat, but some were fortunately reprieved. Other areas were not so lucky. It is hoped that this collection of photographs revive pleasant memories for some, and for younger people give a glimpse of an era when railways were not only a viable alternative but, for most people, the only way to travel.

Bodmin North — Wadebridge

Passenger service withdrawn	30 January 1967
Distance	6.6 miles
Company	Bodmin & Wadebridge Railway

Stations closed	*Date*
Bodmin North	30 January 1967
Grogley Halt	30 January 1967

Stations closed	*Date*
Nanstallon Halt	30 January 1967
Dunmere Halt	30 January 1967
Shooting Range Platform *	1947

* One and a half miles from Wadebridge, this was restricted to military use.

Bodmin North Station. The steam railmotor was built in 1906 but these were underpowered and had difficulty with trailers at peak times. No. 8 was taken out of service in 1915.

Grogley Halt, June 1934. One of three halts opened in 1906 to coincide with the introduction of steam railmotors.

The Bodmin & Wadebridge Railway was built to carry sand (used for agricultural purposes) from the Camel estuary and opened in 1834, when the line to Wenford Bridge was regarded as the mainline and Bodmin was only a branch. In the nineteenth century Bodmin was the county town of Cornwall so it was fitting that it was served by two railways even if they were only branches. With an eye to expansion, the LSWR illegally bought the line in 1846, but it was not linked to the rest of the LSWR system until 1895. Prior to that its only rail connection had been that of the GWR branch to Bodmin (since 1888). The Southern Railway ran frequent services from Bodmin North through Wadebridge to Padstow and its North Cornwall mainline – in the 1920s there were eight trains daily between Bodmin and Wadebridge.

The level crossing and halt at Nanstallon, January 1937.

Dunmere Halt, 1947. The halts on this line all had corrugated iron pagoda-style waiting huts which are more often associated with the GWR.

Bodmin Road — Bodmin General

Passenger service withdrawn	30 January 1967	*Stations closed*	*Date*
Distance	3.5 miles	Bodmin General	30 January 1967
Company	Great Western Railway		

This line was built as a standard gauge line and opened on 27 May 1887. It was extended to join the Bodmin & Wadebridge Railway at Boscarne Junction in September 1888, a distance of 2.7 miles. Services then ran both to Bodmin Road and over LSWR metals to Wadebridge. After closure Bodmin General steam shed was a centre for the Great Western Society for a number of years. More recently the line from Bodmin Road (now known as Bodmin Parkway) has been taken over by a preservation society. It is known as the Bodmin & Wenford Railway and operates both steam and diesel trains to Bodmin and Boscarne Junction.

Bude branch *

Passenger service withdrawn	1 October 1966	*Stations closed*	*Date*
Distance	18.5 miles	Bude	1 October 1966
Company	Devon & Cornwall Railway/		
	London & South Western Railway		

Although Bude Station was on the outskirts of town, the waiting carriages undoubtedly did a good trade.

The Devon & Cornwall Railway commenced building its branch to Holsworthy from Meldon Junction in 1875 and it was opened on 20 January 1879. When the line was opened Beaworthy was an intermediate station (it was later renamed Halwill and Beaworthy, then Halwill Junction, and still later Halwill (for Beaworthy)). Like the people of Padstow, Bude had to wait a long time for a rail connection – the extension was not opened by the LSWR until 10 August 1898. This section needed a nine arch viaduct which was built in concrete and predates the better known Glenfinnan viaduct in Scotland, built by Bob McAlpine, by about two years. Only the last 4.5 miles of the branch was in Cornwall and Bude was the only Cornish station. Bude had an earlier flirtation with modern transport in the shape of the Bude Canal which mainly transported sand to improve the poor soil of inland farms. A branch was built down to the canal basin and the railway took much of the canal's traffic. When the North Cornwall line opened the line to Bude was worked as a branch from Halwill. On a summer Saturday in Southern days Bude had its own portion of the Atlantic Coast Express originating at Waterloo, but by the 1960s a DMU sufficed.

* Closed stations on this line that were in Devon were Whitstone & Bridgerule, Holsworthy, and Dunsland Cross.

Chacewater (Blackwater Junction) — Newquay (Tolcarne Junction)

Passenger service withdrawn	4 February 1963	*Stations closed*	*Date*
Distance	18.5 miles	Mithian Halt	4 February 1963
Company	Great Western Railway	Perranporth Beach Halt	4 February 1963
		Perranporth	4 February 1963
Stations closed	*Date*	Goonhavern	4 February 1963
Mount Hawke Halt	4 February 1963	Shepherds	4 February 1963
St Agnes	4 February 1963	Mitchell and Newlyn Halt	4 February 1963
Goonbell Halt	4 February 1963	Trewerry and Trerice Halt	4 February 1963

Mount Hawke Halt, looking north, 1922.

The first St Agnes Station, photographed before the First World War. It was rebuilt with an island platform on the same site in 1937.

This line opened in two sections: from Chacewater to Perranporth on 6 July 1903, and from Perranporth to Newquay on 2 January 1905. Newquay, a prominent resort on the north coast of Cornwall, had been served by rail for some time before this branch was built. The Cornwall Minerals Railway opened in June 1874 and part of that company's line was incorporated into the Perranporth to Newquay section. The CMR line, via its junction at Par, made a quicker route to Plymouth and London and in later days this became (and still is) the route for holidaymakers to Newquay. Despite this the branch from Chacewater provided a useful link to mid and west Cornwall; through services ran to Truro and, by means of a triangular junction at Blackwater, to west Cornwall in the summer only (this service was withdrawn in September 1916). Passenger traffic could be light in winter and the line was operated at times by GWR steam railmotors. Acknowledgment of Perranporth's development as a resort came with the provision of Perranporth Beach Halt in July 1931.

Goonbell Halt, looking west, 1922.

Mithian Halt, looking south, 1922. This and the other halts on the line all opened in 1905.

G.W.R. STATION, PERRANPORTH. No 1.

Perranporth Station, photographed soon after it was opened in 1903. In the foreground, sheeted over, is a portable engine. This would probably have been used for agricultural purposes such as driving a threshing machine.

Perranporth Station, May 1960. No. 4593 was one of the 4575 class of Prairie tanks built at Swindon in 1927.

Goonhavern Halt, 1922.

Trewerry and Trerice Halt, 1922.

(Blackwater West Loop)

Passenger service withdrawn   September 1916   *Distance*   0.2 miles

This is the line mentioned on page 10 that gave direct access from Newquay to west Cornwall. There were no stations on it.

Gwinear Road — Helston

Passenger service withdrawn	3 November 1962	*Stations closed*	*Date*
Distance	8.8 miles	Praze	3 November 1962
Company	Helston Railway	Nancegollan	3 November 1962
		Truthall Platform	3 November 1962
		Helston	3 November 1962

The water tower at Praze Station, 1905. The chimneys of the station building can be seen behind the steam railmotor which could be no. 24 as this is known to have been used on the Chacewater–Newquay branch.

The staff of Praze Station seem to be more interested in the photographer than the approaching Helston train.

The Helston branch line opened on 9 May 1887 after several abortive attempts to provide a rail link to this important tin mining and market town, the commercial and business centre for The Lizard. These included, in 1864, the grandly named Cornwall Union Railway which was intended to link Helston to Penryn and Penzance and Penzance to St Just (in Penwith). The line was worked by the GWR and was absorbed by that company in 1898. In August 1903 the GWR introduced its first omnibus service, from Helston to The Lizard, using Milnes-Daimler buses previously used by the Lynton & Barnstaple Railway between Ilfracombe and Blackmoor Station on that railway. The line was never of great importance for holidaymakers, but carried passengers and general freight including heavy cauliflower traffic when the crop was in season. On 8 May each year considerable extra traffic was provided by the annual Floral Dance. After the Second World War a naval air station opened at Culdrose near Helston, but despite some extra traffic from this the line was the first in Cornwall to close under the Beeching Plan.

No. 5515 at Nancegollan Station, August 1961. This was the only crossing place on the branch. There is a lot of freight in the yard, but despite this the line closed completely in October 1964.

Truthall Platform, 1920. This stopping place was opened in July 1905 and was known as Truthall Halt until July 1906.

Helston Station, which was the most southerly in Britain, pictured in 1920. Although this station closed in 1962, the locomotive shed remained in use until December the following year.

No. 4545 at Helston, not long before the station closed. Goods services continued until October 1964.

Hayle Railway

Passenger service withdrawn	16 February 1852	Stations closed	Date
Distance	9.5 miles	Angarrack	16 February 1852
Company	Hayle Railway	Gwinear	16 February 1852
		Penponds	16 February 1852
Stations closed	Date	Camborne *	16 February 1852
Hayle	16 February 1852	Pool **	16 February 1852
Copperhouse	16 February 1852	Redruth	16 February 1852

The Hayle Railway was authorised in 1834, opening for goods in 1837 and for passengers in May 1843 to the Stephenson gauge of 4 feet 8½ inches. It was originally proposed to provide transport to the mining district of Camborne-Redruth, in the same way as the Redruth and Chasewater line did via the southern port of Devoran. However, the Hayle Railway had the advantage of using locomotives from the beginning (the Redruth and Chasewater line used horses until 1854, after which locomotives took over). Travelling on the Hayle Railway was an adventurous trip as an incline was involved at Angarrack and on at least one occasion the wire rope broke. Fortunately the coaches ran back to Hayle and the passengers returned to their starting point rather shaken but otherwise unhurt. It provided a passenger service from Hayle to Redruth from May 1843 until the advent of the West Cornwall Railway, which took over the Hayle Railway and extended it eastwards to Truro and westwards to Penzance, opening throughout in August 1852.

* Reopened March 1852 as part of the West Cornwall Railway.   ** Reopened and renamed Carn Brea as part of the West Cornwall Railway, August 1852.

Launceston branch *

			Date
Passenger service withdrawn	29 December 1962	*Stations closed*	
Distance	32 miles	Launceston North	30 June 1952
Company	Launceston & South Devon Railway		

Launceston was long regarded as the gateway to Cornwall but its status suffered when it was bypassed by the first railways into the county. This broad gauge line was an extension of the line to Tavistock and was built by the LSDR, opening in 1865. During the Second World War a junction was put in between the GWR and Southern lines at Launceston and Western Region trains ran over this into the Southern station after Launceston (GWR) closed on 30 June 1952. The last train on the line should have been the 8.35 p.m. departure from Launceston, but the previous train had encountered heavy snowfalls, arriving in Plymouth three hours behind time, and the 6.30 p.m. Plymouth to Launceston got to Tavistock at 12.25 a.m., more than five hours late. So Launceston never saw its last trains. Today the only railway in Launceston is the Launceston Steam Railway, a two foot gauge line running over part of the old Southern trackbed. It is well worth visiting.

* Other closed stations on the branch that were in Devon were Marsh Mills, Plym Bridge, Bickleigh, Shaugh Bridge Platform, Clearbrook Halt, Yelverton, Horrabridge, Whitchurch Down Platform, Tavistock South, Mary Tavy & Blackdown, Lydford, Liddaton Halt, Coryton, and Lifton.

Lostwithiel — Fowey

			Date
Passenger service withdrawn	4 January 1965	*Stations closed*	
Distance	5.4 miles	Golant	4 January 1965
Company	Cornwall Minerals Railway	Fowey	4 January 1965

Golant, looking towards Lostwithiel, 1922.

Fowey Station, 1922. The line to the left of the photograph was from St Blazey. It ran through the station and on to Lostwithiel.

The Lostwithiel & Fowey Railway built a broad gauge line to Carne Point. It carried china clay for shipment by sea but became engaged in such ruinous competition with the Cornwall Minerals Railway line that it closed on 1 January 1880. After reconstruction and extension by the CMR (which had, itself, been worked by the GWR since October 1877) it reopened as a standard gauge line in September 1895, to all intents and purposes a GWR branch as it now carried passengers and the extension took it to the CMR station in Fowey. The line was operated by railmotors for a while and later became the only Cornish branch worked by the classic GWR autotrain. China clay trains still run to the loading jetties at Fowey, but passenger traffic ceased in January 1965.

Newham branch

Passenger service withdrawn	16 September 1863	*Stations closed*	*Date*
Distance	2.4 miles	Newham	16 September 1863
Company	West Cornwall Railway		

This was the Truro terminus of the West Cornwall Railway (although there had been an earlier temporary station at Truro Road) and ran from Penwithers Junction. It saw little traffic after the Cornwall Railway made a connection with the West Cornwall in 1859.

North Cornwall line *

Passenger service withdrawn	3 October 1966	*Stations closed*	*Date*
Distance	48.6 miles	Otterham	3 October 1966
Company	North Cornwall Railway	Camelford	3 October 1966
		Delabole	3 October 1966
Stations closed	*Date*	Port Isaac Road	3 October 1966
Launceston	3 October 1966	St Kew Highway	3 October 1966
Egloskerry	3 October 1966	Wadebridge	28 January 1967
Tresmeer	3 October 1966	Padstow	28 January 1967

Otterham Station. Built at an altitude of 850 feet, this station was often subject to gales that blew in from the nearby Atlantic.

* The closed stations on this line that were in Devon were Ashwater and Tower Hill.

Camelford Station. The town of Camelford was 1½ miles away and trains were met by horse buses in the early days, although motor buses were used later.

In the 1840s the LSWR had cherished ambitions of opening a line to Truro and Falmouth, via Bodmin, but these were never realised. Its link to the isolated Bodmin & Wadebridge Railway was completed much later. The jubilant people of Padstow rang church bells after a meeting in 1881 at which funds towards the NCR survey were offered, but they were to wait almost twenty years for the link to become a reality. The NCR was promoted as a separate company (it remained a separate entity until 1922) that the LSWR was to work and the appropriate Act was passed in 1882. The construction was so drawn out that several additional acts were needed. The line was opened in six sections: Halwill to Launceston, 20 July 1886; Launceston to Tresmeer, 28 July 1892; Tresmeer to Camelford, 14 August 1893; Camelford to Delabole, 18 October 1893; Delabole to Wadebridge, 1 June 1895; and Wadebridge to Padstow, 24 March 1899. The North Cornwall line commenced at Halwill Junction in Devon and headed south to Launceston in Cornwall before passing north of Bodmin Moor to Wadebridge and a terminus at Padstow. The line was always considered as a mainline by the LSWR and the Southern even though the entire Southern system west of Exeter was known as 'The Withered Arm'. It was a boost to the tourist trade of north Cornwall and its famous train, the Atlantic Coast Express, commenced in 1926. The 'Woolworth' 2-6-0s arrived on the line in 1924 and were to be regular performers almost until the line's closure. Bulleid Light Pacifics – the 'West Country' and 'Battle of Britain' classes – arrived in 1945.

Delabole Station.

Port Isaac Road Station, August 1962. Apart from the station signs and the road vehicles in the background, there is little to suggest that this is not pre-grouping days.

Wadebridge Station, 1913. The station building is still extant and is now the John Betjeman Centre for the Retired.

Wadebridge Station, 1895. At this date Wadebridge was a terminus. It was rebuilt as a three platform station in 1899.

Wadebridge Station. This picture shows the island platform and in the background is a steam railmotor; the last of these was withdrawn from Wadebridge in 1918.

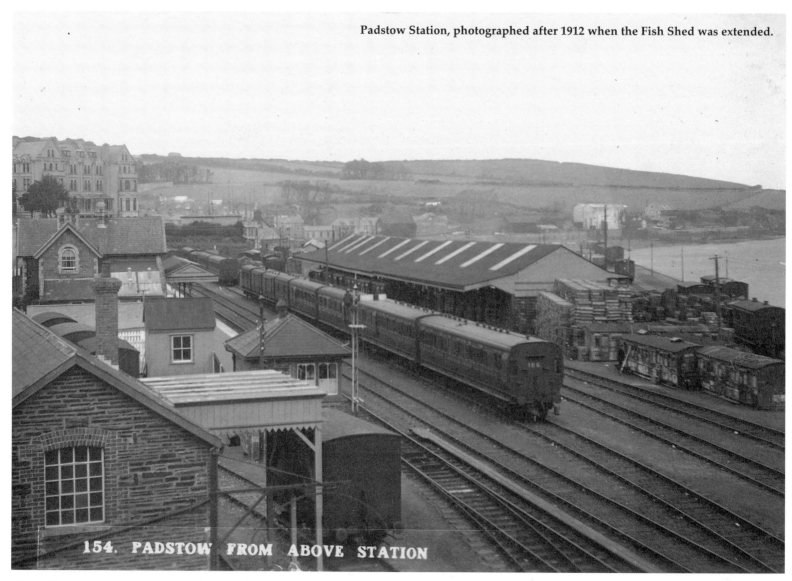

Padstow Station, photographed after 1912 when the Fish Shed was extended.

154. PADSTOW FROM ABOVE STATION

Assembled worthies await the arrival of the director's special train for the opening ceremony of Padstow Station, 23 March 1899. In the best traditions of such ceremonies, the band played 'See the Conquering Hero Comes'.

Plymouth, Devonport & South Western Junction Railway: Callington branch

Passenger service withdrawn	5 November 1966		*Stations closed*	*Date*
Distance (closed section)	5 miles		Seven Stones	5 November 1966
Company Plymouth, Devon & South Western Junction Railway			Luckett *	5 November 1966
			Callington	5 November 1966

Stations closed	*Date*
Chilsworthy	5 November 1966
Latchley	5 November 1966

* Known as Stoke Climsland until 1 November 1909.

Chilsworthy Station, July 1949.

Luckett Station (previously called Stoke Climsland).

Stoke Climsland Station

Running from Bere Alston to Callington, this line was known as the Callington section of the PD&SWJR. It had similarities with the North Devon & Cornwall Junction Light Railway: part of it was built on the track of the 3 feet 6 inch gauge East Cornwall Minerals Railway and its engineer was the same as that railway's, H.F. Stephens. Unlike its mainline from Lydford to Plymouth, which was always worked by the LSWR, the company worked its own trains through to Plymouth and its loco stock included a pair of handsome Hawthorn Leslie 0-6-2Ts. It was taken over by the LSWR in 1922. The line opened in 1908 and crossed the Tamar on a magnificent viaduct which had a wagon lift to enable mineral traffic to reach the wharves at Calstock, avoiding an earlier incline. When closure threatened in the 1960s the section to Gunnislake was retained, at least part of the reason being to give a crossing over the River Tamar at this point, and a delightful ride along the Tamar and over the lofty viaduct is still possible.

A view of the engine shed at Callington Station, taken from the end of the platform. The photograph probably dates from before the First World War.

Callington Station.

One of the line's original Hawthorn-Leslie 0-6-2Ts, 'Earl St Leven', at
Callington Station. The station's overall roof can be seen in the background.

St Blazey — Fowey

Passenger service withdrawn	8 July 1929	*Stations closed*	*Date*
Distance	4.5 miles	St Blazey	21 September 1925
Company	Cornwall Minerals Railway		

St Blazey Station, 1922, looking towards Newquay. Note the row of china clay wagons behind the station.

Opened originally as part of the CMR's mainline from Fowey to Newquay in June 1874, passenger services commenced on 20 June 1876. It became part of the GWR on 1 July 1896, having been worked by that company since 1 October 1877. The route included the Pinnock tunnel which, at 1,173 yards, was the longest in Cornwall. On 1 January 1870 the curve from St Blazey to Par was opened and from that date all CMR trains, both to Newquay and Fowey, ran to and from Par, necessitating a reversal at St Blazey for the Fowey trains. The Cornwall Minerals Railway had been built to the Stephenson gauge of 4 feet 8½ inches (standard gauge) so through running was not possible until 1892. In the 1920s the two routes provided Fowey with ten passenger trains a day, pretty good for a Cornish fishing port. This line remained open for china clay traffic until August 1968. Subsequently a private road has been built over the line for trucks to carry the clay (the road also goes through the Pinnock tunnel).

Closed passenger stations on lines still open to passengers

Line/service	Liskeard–Looe	Stations closed	Date
Stations closed	Date	Chacewater	5 October 1964
Moorswater	15 May 1901	Truro Road **	16 April 1855
		Probus & Ladock	2 December 1957
		Grampound Road	5 October 1964
Line/service	Penzance–Plymouth	Burngullow (1st station)	1 August 1901
Stations closed	Date	Burngullow (2nd station)	14 September 1931
Marazion	5 October 1964	Doublebois	5 October 1964
Gwinear Road	5 October 1964	Defiance Platform	27 October 1930
Carn Brea	2 January 1961		
Scorrier *	5 October 1964		

Gwinear Road Station, 1920, looking towards Penzance. Although passenger service here ceased in 1964, goods traffic continued until August 1965.

* Originally named Scorrier Gate until 1856 when it was renamed as Scorrier. From 1859 until October 1896 it went back to being Scorrier Gate before becoming simply Scorrier once more.

** This served as the West Cornwall Railway terminus until the extension to Newham opened.

No. 4095, 'Harlech Castle', at Gwinear Road, August 1958. This engine was built in June 1926 and withdrawn in December 1962.

Carn Brea Station, 1922, looking towards Penzance. Carn Brea was the site of the West Cornwall Railway workshops and a number of locomotives were built there.

Scorrier Station, looking towards Truro. The signalbox here opened in 1902 and was closed in 1930.

Scorrier, 1920, again looking towards Truro. The milk churns on the platform are a reminder of how the railways used to supply towns and cities with milk.

No. 4565 with the Newquay train at Chacewater, August 1958. This engine was one of the original 45XX series of locomotives with small tanks, built at Swindon in 1924.

**Probus & Ladock Platform, May 1922, looking towards Plymouth.
This stopping place opened in February 1908.**

Grampound Road Station, looking towards Penzance. This station was the railhead for a large area but was almost two miles from Grampound itself.

GRAMPOUND ROAD STATION

The second Burngullow Station, 1922, looking towards Penzance. The line to the right was the china clay line to Drinnick Mill and St Dennis Junction on the Par–Newquay line. Further to the right is the track to the engine shed which closed in April 1922. The track looks to have been a survivor from the broad gauge days, having been slewed in to 4 feet, 8½ inches.

Doublebois Station, 1947, looking towards Plymouth. The siding to the right was one of a number put in by the War Department in 1943.